Grief: The Spoken Words

Alexis Bonavitacola
Artwork and illustrations by Bil Donovan

Grief: The Spoken Words

Publisher: Alexis Bonavitacola Press
Philadelphia, PA, United States
stillholdinggrief.com

ISBNs
Paperback: 979-8-9934523-3-3
eBook: 979-8-9934523-4-0

Credits
Cover design: Bil Donovan
Interior layout & typography: Hamza Hashmi
Artwork & illustrations: Bil Donovan

First Edition
Printed in the United States of America

CONTENTS

GRIEF: THE SPOKEN WORDS
A Poetry Collection

Companion to the memoir
Holding On After Goodbye:
A Memoir of Sibling Loss,
Carrying Grief, and What Endures

ALEXIS BONAVITACOLA

Foreword

"Take your little sister with you, mommy and daddy used to tell you", Alexis said, standing on the altar to begin her eulogy for her older brother Kenny. "And you did. You brought me everywhere." As her husband, I knew how hard this was for her.

Toward the end of March 2025, I had just walked home after getting a haircut, and as I approached our house, Alexis was outside waiting for me: "John," she said with tears in her eyes, "something terrible has happened." *She* told me her brother Kenny was in the hospital in New York City. It was a shock to everyone who loved him. It was catastrophic to her when he died within two weeks from pancreatic cancer.

When I watched them together over the last twenty years, there were times when Kenny still seemed to be holding her hand, and when I listened to them, I could visualize the young boy leading the young girl through the early days of her life. They were only eighteen months apart. And as she moved on through the dance of life, he was always there, holding her hand.

As I listened to Alexis' eulogy, each word to her brother went forth imbued in the tone of grief. The words reflected her suffering; the suffering I had watched day after day, coming at her unpredictably, like a straight-line wind of emotional pain.

***

Hemingway said it best in a letter to a parent who had lost a child: *No one you love is ever dead.* And so Kenny's death, which has become a crucible for her as it intrudes into every facet of her being, implored her to write this book. Alexis didn't do it because of a literary aspiration or a goal of becoming a published author.

She created it because of the multidimensional impact of grief.

In doing so, she was able to "carve" out a balancing act between the ordeal of her grief for Kenny and the memories of who he was and what he was to her. It was cathartic for her; and I believe with all my heart, so it will be for any reader who has experienced the loss of a loved one.

I am so proud of her achievement...and even more proud that although she still struggles, she found a way to alleviate at least some of the pain of Kenny's loss. It is so clear on every page of this stunning book.

John Paterna

Prologue

grief is not quiet
but we are taught to be

we lower our eyes
we change the subject
we offer one careful sentence
and hope someone hears
what we cannot say

these spoken words are for the places grief goes

when the room falls silent
in our cars at red lights
in our kitchens at midnight
the space between sleeping and waking
where sorrow lives

grief is not linear
it circles back
surprises us
lives in the ordinary days
that will never be ordinary again

some of these poems first lived in my memoir
Holding On After Goodbye:
A Memoir of Sibling Loss, Carrying Grief, and
What Endures

many were written in the raw days after loss
when breathing felt impossible

others arrived later
when love refused to stay quiet
when grief demanded a voice

if you have been carrying your sorrow in silence
let these words keep you company

you are not alone in the weight you carry

your grief has a place here

your love deserves to be spoken

UNIMAGINABLE LOSS

ALEXIS BONAVITACOLA

grief is a doorway

you never meant to open
never thought you'd have to

but one day
without warning
you're standing in its frame

hands trembling on either side
unsure whether to go back
or forward

on this side
the life you knew
the person you were
still hearing his voice

on the other
a silence
you don't yet know how to live with

you cross anyway
because you must

and when you do
you learn to carry absence
like a shadow that lengthens
as the days wear on

grief is a doorway

~~~~~

on the other side

the self
you never imagined
becoming

no ordinary day

it wasn't marked
as the day my heart would break

i only wrote
call mom
gym
supermarket

like the future
still existed

what i didn't know

he didn't tell me

he kept the cancer
unspoken until

it was too much to hold
too heavy to keep inside

later he confessed
he knew it would kill me too

he tried to protect me
from the impending loss
from time running out
from knowing too soon
that goodbye was already near

and i am grateful

and i am furious

and i understand

and i don't

too tired

he looked at me
not with fear
not with pain

just the weight of everything

the way someone looks
when they know
the next breath may be too much

he said my name
like he was placing it down

gently

so it wouldn't break

her job

she sat beside him
adjusting ice packs
reading messages from people who loved him

she'd text me after
careful to echo his words
into the perfect emoji

it was the one thing she could still give

his voice carried through her fingertips
with a soft edge of humor
she'd write me
i love my job

but it was never a job

it was love
being his voice
when his own grew quiet

when words failed
he'd lift his eyes
point to the phone
so she could read what love still carried to him

a bridge to his heart
from those reaching for him

in those final days
she found one quiet space
where he could still be himself

responding to friends
held by the love around him

it didn't look heroic

but it meant everything

everything
to him

each other's heroes

a chair pulled close
a hand held tightly

nothing left to fix

you're my hero
a voice whispered in the dark

no

the hand squeezed back

you're mine

no grandness
only truth

the courage to let go

the trust to carry on

two brothers

one vigil

each other's heroes

the last sense to go

they say he could still hear me
even sedated
even then

but i didn't whisper
didn't say anything

i froze beside the bed
searching every inch
of his face
for signs of return

but he'd already left me

now speak to him
i scream for him

in my dreams
in the shower
in my car
on the page
everywhere

into the deafening silence
into the absence

and i pray

please hear me now

our last acts of love

grief sat beside us
silent and heavy

while we chose the urn
the songs
the photos

gluing your life
onto poster boards

we wrote the words
to speak to hundreds

opened doors
said thank you
crumbled into embraces

if we couldn't save you
we could still care for you
line the church with your pictures
of a life that ended far too soon

we let the tears fall
and say with every small decision

you were here
you mattered

these were our last acts of love

they came for you

one by one
they entered
from every part of your life

they came with tears
and trembling hands
with memories tucked into their hearts
with grief too big for words

some i hadn't seen in decades
their arrival shattered my composure
because they didn't have to come
but they did
for you
for us

they weren't silent

they shared stories
of how much you gave

each embrace reminded me
you were loved
by so many
not just by us

and something happened in that room

in the depth of grief
the strength of love rose up
your light still shining

in every story

every tear
every person who said
you made them feel seen

you softened hard days
you made people feel special
you made us feel everything

seen

held

loved

consolation

they say

aren't you glad he didn't suffer
he went fast
he spared you the pain of watching
him die

how can i say no to this

when didn't want it to happen
in the first place

they say

this should give you consolation
how

when i still ask

why

no time to prepare

suddenly
you were gone

no time to prepare
for a world
without my brother

the pain
the loss

unbearable

forever changed

our family
forever changed

no longer four
just three now

every new picture
every frame
your absence
leans heavy
against us

the missing shoulder
the shape of you
we still reach for

centering us

anchoring us

i wish i told you

i wish i told you
to find a way to fight
to want to stay
to not give in

i wish i told you
that even though
you can't
take me with you

when you die

you're not letting go
you're bringing me with you

because

i'm dying too

i am not strong

please don't want me to be

let me break
into a million little pieces

i can't be put back together

it doesn't feel real

i read your death certificate
i have all your belongings

your urn
filled with ashes
with you

we talk of you in past tense

i still can't believe
it's true

it's real

THE CARRYING

ALEXIS BONAVITACOLA

unreachable

you slipped into the horizon of my life
and every day since

i've been swimming toward the shape of you

unmoored

———⌐ↄ☊ↄↄ¬———

grief unhooks you from the shore

it snaps the lines you didn't even know were tethering
you

the daily check-ins
the inside jokes
the way your world used to feel held

now everything drifts

the days blur
the calendar doesn't make sense
your body moves
but your soul feels somewhere else

adrift

you start searching for new ropes
to anchor you

routine
writing
ritual

anything that might hold you still
for even a moment

some days you feel like you're floating toward something
other days you feel like you're just lost at sea

but maybe
maybe

grief is the ocean

and you're learning to swim

when routine falls apart

i had appointments that week written down

haircut.
exercise
taxes
notes about projects

all of it still there
quietly irrelevant
what wasn't written down
- call the undertaker
- call the priest
- try to reach everyone who ever loved him
- find the words to say it out loud
- *he's dying*
- say goodbye
there are no sticky notes for that

no checkboxes for heartbreak

no reminder that says
today, your world will split in two

grief didn't just take you

it moved everything you touched

suddenly
nothing in my life was where i left it

what grief does

grief strips everything down
to its essence

it lays you bare

it shows up and asks you to feel
what you never imagined

it burns away
everything unnecessary

until only this remains

two simple words
you died

fine thank you

———— ৩৭৬ ————

how are you

i'm fine
thank you

but, i'm not

no one sees

that I'm holding back
a thousand unsaid words
for my brother

for a single name
i still can't say
without breaking

if you really want to know
i still can't believe he's gone

every quiet moment in my head
is filled with thoughts of him
an endless loop of his smile
laughter
texts
phone calls
Facebook posts

his presence
letting me know every day
he was here

and now he's not

the pain of longing

grief gives you pain
you never imagined
you could feel

as if someone replaced
everything inside you
with something heavier

made entirely of longing

a constant ache

i didn't know pain
could be this complete

this permanent

sometimes i miss

sometimes i miss
those immediate days
after he died
his name spoken constantly
stories and memories pouring out
long embraces
tears
comfort
kindness
endless offers
anything you need.
as gut-wrenching as those days were
we were cradled
by the love of everyone
who cherished him
he was everywhere
in every story
every hug
every tear
every person who showed up
his absence was filled
with so much visible love
that
in a strange way

he felt more present
than gone
but then the visits stopped
and the calls grew quiet

and grief
moved in
for good

you think you know

you think you know
what unimaginable grief
will feel like

but

it's impossible to
anticipate

until you get there

the paradox of grief

in darkness we seek light

feel everything
and nothing

we want to forget the pain
but never the person

grief

all contradictions

shelf life

grief feels like it comes
with an expiration date

like a carton of milk
best if used within 30 days

and you start to feel it

the unspoken timeline
no one says it directly
but you feel the expectation

shouldn't you be over it by now

you start to monitor yourself
count the moments since you last cried

wonder if talking about him
makes people uncomfortable

feel ashamed for still aching
still naming the loss out loud

because hasn't the shelf life
on your grief expired by now

and then you start to believe it
you begin to feel
like your grief
is taking up too much room
lasting too long

asking too much

of a world that's moved on

just because

just because you see me functioning
just because you see me smiling
just because you see me whole
doesn't mean i'm not aching

you don't see me curled up

weeping for my person

the one

who left me far too soon

when you start hiding it

at some point
you stop saying how much it hurts

not because it hurts less
but because the people around you
start hurting more
when you say it out loud

you protect them
you downplay the heaviness

you change the subject

you cry in the car instead
you smile so they won't worry
you act okay
so they don't fall apart

you become great at passing as fine
even when you're barely standing

you love them too much
to hand them the full weight of your grief

you carry it quietly

but hiding grief
doesn't make it disappear

it just makes you disappear

quicksand

i've only ever seen quicksand
in movies

someone trapped
slowly going under

it always terrified me
like drowning
but slower
not because you don't try

but because you do

in quicksand
movement pulls you deeper
fighting makes it worse

the more you panic
the more you sink

and that's how it feels
every day
all day

the weight
the pull
the helpless effort

i am trying
and still

i sink

the language of grief

grief is a language
most people never learn

so they don't know the words
for staying
when your sorrow lasts too long
for their comfort

adrift in the fog

it hurts the most when
the numbness has worn off
the shock is gone
the loss is real
permanent

and it starts to live in strange places

in the grocery store
in the driveway
in your own reflection
it shows up in Home Goods
when you lose your cart
twice
because you couldn't think straight
couldn't remember what aisle you had been in
just standing there
adrift among throw pillows and coffee mugs

holding back tears
through the fog of grief

and when you cry now
you feel like you must apologize for it
as if grief should have packed up

and left by now

what you need

you just need someone to sit beside you
and say

does it still hurt

then I'm still listening

pandora's box

people are afraid
to open the box of my grief

if they don't ask
or mention his name
all the sadness will stay contained

but their silence
causes the real pain

the isolation

the feeling that his absence
is too uncomfortable to acknowledge

their curiosity about my sorrow
something terrible

but it's their fear
that keeps the box sealed

i wish they knew

opening it would let his light out
let me speak his name
let his love fill the room

let me heal

grief is not chaos to contain
it's loss asking to be shared

anything

what i wish they'd say......
anything

anything but silence

what to say instead

when someone is grieving
we often say
"i'm so sorry for your loss

it's kind
it's heartfelt

but it can also feel
like the end of the conversation
a full stop

and grief rarely wants silence

sometimes what someone truly needs
is not sympathy
but invitation

tell me about them
what did you love most

open a conversation

it gives space to speak their loved one's name
to share memories that are still alive inside them

it shifts the moment from pain
to presence

from loss
to love

being present
genuinely present
means listening

sitting with their ache
quietly

honoring the love they carry

smile

grief taught me to wear a smile
so well
even i believed it

flawless
practiced
deceiving

grief reveals

some people surprise you
with their absence

grief reveals

some friendships
don't survive your grief

but your capacity for empathy
for compassion
for holding space for others

that grows

and softens the edges of someone else's
pain
someone else's
grief

hold

i am
holding on
and
holding back
and
holding in
and
holding up

i hold the grief

because i can't let it go

and because

it won't let go of me

WHAT REMAINS

ALEXIS BONAVITACOLA

angels

they were there
when he was sick
when he was scared
when he couldn't tell us
they knew
before we did

they sat by his side
held his hand
made sure he was never alone

they buried others
stood graveside
hearts shattered from AIDS

still they rose
again
and again

to show up
to love
to not look away

they cleaned his apartment
gathered his things
folded the fabrics of his life
so i wouldn't have to
so i could simply arrive

numb
in his space

to grieve

and take what was left

they were his family

before we knew
before we understood
how much of him they carried
they were

his angels

and now
they are mine

afraid to look

people tell me often that i'll heal
that i'll get over this pain
that i'll move on
carry only the wonderful memories
and one day laugh again
when i see a photo or a video of your beautiful face

but they don't understand

when i'm deep in the trenches of grief
it feels less like healing
and more like suffocating

grief becomes a wall closing in
each breath tighter than the last

even lifting my head feels dangerous
because i don't want to look at a world
where you no longer exist

healing feels like a foreign language
no one ever taught me how to speak
the only words i know how to say are

he's gone

his winter coat

not just fabric
but form

not just warmth
but weight

not just his
but mine now

i lift it
and it holds me
more than i hold it

the scent

faint
fading
still there

like memory

like love

like him

still here

your picture is still on my phone
your smile shows up whenever i send a text
you're still in my favorites
because how could i ever remove you

every time i scroll
i find another piece of you

the way you checked in
the way we loved each other in words

your last texts still haunt me
you were dying
and still loving me

i can't imagine a time
when i won't want to see you
won't want to read those messages
again

and again

and again

like twins

today someone said
you were like twins

i'd never thought of it that way

but maybe that's why
this grief feels like amputation
like i've been split in half
and left to balance
on memory alone

i wonder what conjoined twins feel
when separated
if their bodies ache
for what used to be attached

if their minds reach
for what's missing
even when they try not to

because since you left
nothing holds me up
the way it used to

my other half

is gone

the keeper of his stories

now it's my turn

to keep the circle unbroken
to hold the stories he once gave us
and place them back on the table

i carry his voice forward

sometimes afraid the details will fade

but for now they live in me
and when i tell them
it feels like he's here again
gathering us close

with one more story

not a day goes by

not a day goes by
not a single day
without saying your name
without you being my first thought each morning
without you being my last thought each night

not a day goes by
without asking why

even though silence always answers

not a day goes by
without the world feeling wrong
not a day goes by that doesn't hurt

not a day goes by

not a single day

the one in your corner

there's always one person
the one who shows up
who sees you

not just when it's easy
but when it's hard

the one who sees you
all of you

the one who reminds you
you're worthy
when the world tries to say otherwise

there's always one person
who makes you feel safe
in your skin

you don't always realize
what that means
until they're gone

and then grief becomes something more
not just sorrow
but disorientation

because when the one in your corner
isn't there anymore

when the one in your corner is gone
you don't just miss them

you miss the version of you
that felt most at home

in their presence

the little things

——— ༄ ༄ ༄ ———

people expect me to miss the big things
birthdays
holidays
celebrations
and i do

but i feel your absence most
in the small things

my texts to you
do you want a salad for dinner
need me to pick you up from the bus
do you have a minute to chat
the door's unlocked
just come in

that was our rhythm
ordinary
easy
open
caring

i still scroll through our messages
the ones no one else would think to save

i didn't know how precious
the little things were

now i write messages in my head
i wait for your text that never comes
the door is still unlocked

but you never walk in

secrets

you were the keeper of my secrets
when i couldn't tell anyone else

not even myself

i turned to you

you didn't flinch
you didn't judge
you listened

you were my vault
my shelter
the one who held
what the world might mishandle

even without words
you knew what i meant

you translated silence
and tears

you calmed me
steadied me
reminded me
that everything could be okay

even when we both knew
it might not
you didn't just keep my secrets

you kept me

photographs

the boxes are filled
with your old photographs

people
places
moments that mattered to you

i sift through them slowly
touching each one
knowing how these mattered to you

there's joy here
evidence of your beautiful life

but with every smile i see
i remember

there will never be another photo of you

not another birthday
not another vacation
not another moment frozen in time

only what's already been

only what remains

our sanctuary

my desk is a shrine
where ashes sleep
here
laughter is framed
his face in every photo
his sketches on the wall
my brother
watching me
my guardian angel
holding me
helping me
loving me
this space
sacred
ours

handle with care

⸺ ꙅꙥꙅ ⸺

your name stitched in soft fabric
always in our hearts
she drapes the blanket over the chair
ordinary evenings turned precious
it falls in a triangle
a gentle embrace.
this room is her refuge now
the blanket
a guardian on her first Mother's Day without you
when i rise to leave
her hands move to smooth the blanket
tucking the corner
the way she once tucked you
love doesn't end with death
rituals steady us
we keep caring
still
some losses live in folded corners
creased with care
a mother's love
never out of place

in my dreams

your presence
i feel it

but i can't see you
i can't find you

i scream your name
but the sound
goes nowhere

an echo chamber

i run
i search
i panic

i can no longer breathe

find him

you're just around the corner

but the corner never ends

every night
i reach
and reach

but you're
never
there

just darkness

and the sound

of your name
caught in my throat

gratitude

thank you

for checking in
checking on me
for wanting to know how i'm really feeling
for listening
for not judging
for not telling me how to feel
for not wanting to fix my grief
for being quiet
for opening your heart
for making space for me
for letting my tears flow
with no interruption
for your presence
for holding me
while i try to carry
the weight
of missing him

from the other side of the silence

what i wish i could hear him tell me

you didn't miss anything
you were there for everything that mattered

you loved me enough
you showed up
you saw me

i'm not gone

just not where you can see me

but i'm still here
still holding your hand
still your big brother
always

that's how i know
we'll find each other again

because love is not bound to endings

and neither are we

the shelter of her love

no matter how old i am
i still need my mother's comfort
when grief feels too heavy
to carry alone

even in her own pain
her own unimaginable loss
she finds the strength
to hold mine

she lets me cry

her words try to help me
see past the ache
that he went fast
didn't suffer

but none of that changes
that i never wanted him
to go

she sits in rooms
filled with his absence

yet somehow makes space
for my sorrow too

with her
i can feel
what she must feel

love doesn't end
our bond transcends age

even if not pain

there are moments
when we need to be someone's child again

to find shelter
in the one person
who has loved us
longest

the first birthday after

your birthday
arriving soon
a looming reminder
of what we've just lost

the first
without you

i want to hold back time
no

it's much too soon
i'm not ready
we're not ready

in years past
this day meant
celebrating another year
of your life

now
we gather
to remember
the day you were born
knowing
you are no longer here

candles waiting
lights dimmed

we bow our heads
in reverence
in gratitude

for the gift
of your life

as tears fall
we each make a silent wish

and know

no matter how desperately we wish
for you to return

our deepest wish
will never
ever
come true

but maybe
just maybe
our real wish
isn't for you to come back

maybe it's for you to know
just how very much
you are still loved

and still missed

change of seasons

as the leaves begin to fall
so do my tears

you died in early spring
and summer came
times at the beach
you could no longer enjoy

but somehow the warmth of the sun
kept the chill of your absence
at bay

now autumn arrives

with cold mornings
that bite my face
reminding me
winter is coming

each new day adds distance
from the last time
we were together

each day
each month
adds a new layer of
loss
absence
grief

the seasons still change

but you
are frozen

in spring.

just a song

the music starts
and there it is
chest flooding
grief in my throat
tears that will not quit
i pull over
eyes closed
remembering us
dancing in my living room
you and me

the way it always was
and the way
it will
never be again

it isn't just a song
it's the music of our life

171 days

time does not sand
the edges

the calendar
still ambushes me
with milestones
anniversaries
birthdays
you will never see

there are no moments
when i accept
that you're gone

each time i think of you
a memory
your laughter
your hug
i scream
in silence

your loss
swallows me whole

and each day
pulls you further
and further

away from me

the mask

yesterday
i smiled
shared stories
said i was doing okay

i celebrated you
with careful words
safe memories
that wouldn't break me

in front of them
i wore my mask
so well
they believed it

today
i can barely
lift my head

the performance
drained everything

protecting them
from my grief
protecting myself
from their discomfort

this is the cost
of making others
comfortable
when i can't share
my sorrow

my loss
my pain

today

i pay the price

if love were enough

it would have wrapped itself around you
fierce and unrelenting
driven the illness out
filled every cell with strength
kept you walking beside us

but love

as vast as it was
was not enough
to save you

the price of love

no matter how deep this pain
even if its intensity
lasts the rest of my life
i will carry it
as a reminder
of how much i loved you

if this ache
is the price i pay
for the gift of being your sister

then i will pay it
again
and again
and again

you were the greatest gift of my life

and i would choose you every time
even knowing how this ends

i'm petrified

i'm petrified
of the pain fading
the tears subsiding
the memories of you
no longer causing
sadness
grief

i'm petrified

i'll hold a picture of you
of us
and no longer feel
my heart shattering

i will no longer crumble
at the thought of
no more tomorrows
with us

this grief
i never want
to move past
to move forward
to get over

let me sit in the wreckage
for as long as i want
grief

my blanket of comfort

the last thread
connecting me
to you

What We Learn From Grieving

Now that grief has settled in for good, its permanence feels overwhelming. The world has changed, and I have changed with it.

When we come face to face with grief, as much as we want to go back, that isn't possible.

Grief is a paradox, often within a single breath.

We are shattered by the loss of no more tomorrows and, at once, held by the joy in what we were given.

We are braving the fire in the only way we know how.

Let the tears fall.

No one should ever apologize for loving so deeply.

There is no timeline for our love. Only the life it keeps teaching us to live.

As we change and grow, so does our grief.

I am grieving and I am grateful.

I am grateful for knowing that life is short and every ordinary moment is borrowed time.

I am grateful because grief burns away what is false and what never really mattered.

I am grateful for the compassion and empathy it has given me.

I can understand suffering in ways I never wanted to but somehow needed to.

I am grateful that when I wander too far into the future, grief pulls me back to what is real: this moment. This now. This love.

I am grateful that perfectionism has crumbled under the weight of loss, and I can see beauty in what is broken, including myself.

I am grateful for every single tear, each one proof of the depth of my capacity to love—a love so strong it outlasts death itself.

But gratitude doesn't soften the ache.

I would give back every hard-won perspective if it meant having him here again.

Grief didn't just take my brother from me.

It gave me a different way of being human.

Acknowledgements

To my husband: from the moment we knew Kenny needed us, you moved heaven and earth—clearing my art studio and transforming it into a serene bedroom so he could come home with comfort and dignity. Though he never made it there, I will never forget what you did for him.

I could not have written this book without your quiet, unwavering support as you held me through the worst of grief and gave me the time and space to pour my heart onto these pages.

To my mother: your steadfast belief in this work made its publication possible. Because of you, Kenny's story and the love held in these words can reach those who need it most.

To my brother: thank you for being the shoulder I leaned on while you were grieving too. Your strength steadied me when I could not stand on my own.

To my children and their families: your constant, unconditional love reminded me daily that I was not walking through the darkest days alone.

About The Author

Alexis Bonavitacola, PhD is a writer and artist based in Philadelphia whose work explores love, loss, and the legacies we carry. Her essay "Cedar Woman" received Honorable Mention in the Wild Woman Writing Contest and was published in *Tulip Tree Review*. *Holding On After Goodbye: A Memoir of Sibling Loss, Carrying Grief, and What Endures* is a tribute to her brother, fashion designer Kenny Bonavitacola, and to the community who loved him. A companion audiobook, *Grief: The Spoken Words*, presents spoken selections from the memoir. Alexis spent decades in education before turning her focus to writing. **stillholdinggrief.com**